Cotton Nero A.x

Cotton Nero A.x

The works of the 'Pearl' poet,
retranscribed, *retraced*, *rebelieved*,
consisting of the following poems:

Sir Gawain and the Green Knight
David Hadbawnik

Pearl
Daniel C. Remein

Tidy
Chris Piuma

Patience
Lisa Ampleman

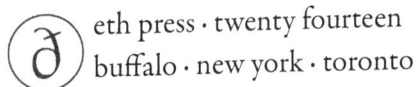

eth press · twenty fourteen
buffalo · new york · toronto

COTTON NERO A.x
© 2014 David Hadbawnik, Daniel C. Remein, Chris Piuma, and Lisa Ampleman.

This work is licensed under a Creative Commons Attribution-NonCommercial 4.0 International License. To view a copy of this license, visit: http://creativecommons.org/licenses/by-nc/4.0/ or send a letter to Creative Commons, 444 Castro Street, Suite 900, Mountain View, California, 94041, USA.

"Sir Gawain and the Green Night" first published in 2011 by Habenicht Press. "Pearl" first published in 2012 by the Organism for Poetic Research.

This edition published in 2014 by
eth press
an imprint of punctum books, Brooklyn, New York
ethpress.com | punctumbooks.com

eth press is a parascholarly poetry press interested in publishing innovative poetry that is inspired by, adapted from, or otherwise inhabited by medieval texts.

eth press is an imprint of punctum books, an open-access and print-on-demand independent publisher dedicated to radically creative modes of intellectual inquiry and writing across a whimsical para-humanities assemblage.

David Hadbawnik, Chris Piuma, and Dan Remein are the editors of eth press, and we can be contacted at ethpress [at] gmail.com. We are currently accepting proposals and submissions.

ISBN-10: 061598391X
ISBN-13: 978-0615983912

Library of Congress Cataloging-in-Publication Data is available from the Library of Congress.

Cover and book design by Chris Piuma.

Sir Gawain and the Green Knight

David Hadbawnik

for Richard Owens

Poker is a game
that depends on the ability
to keep perfectly
devoid of emotion.
Or to fake an emotion—
slight rise of eyebrow
shift in one's seat, fingers
absently fondling chips as
the green knight strolls in

green hair, green coat, converse
all stars painted green-blue. she cuts off
her own head and rolls it
at your astonished feet

Hello
says the head
I have come to warn you—
all of her space between
head and body is simply
meant as a warning—
silently
a bird flies through
a hole in her speech
silently
all of you sitting there
waiting

I keep emptying something
        or
something keeps emptything
        me
blonde   brunette
        redhead
walks out from behind
the counter dark
smock smeared with blood
how can we help you?

The game of poker is symmetrical as a poem, the poem of the green knight. There's nothing left over but a single chip, a smile that dangles in the mind of the last player to fold his or her cards and pick up his or her head from the long green table before strolling out.

Gawain comes into the poem
polite and sloppy as death,
gives up his name,
gives up the ghost
does not pass go
does not make love
to the king through
the lady's body or
any other body who
would not make that mistake

It's imperative to shift
the tongue downward
almost as one would
a glance. Any appendage
tipped in blood, thrumming, this
is the point of the hunt.
Would you like another drink
is not a question Gawain
would know to ask
never having even once
been drunk

The strangest feature of the poem of the green knight is that everything happens at the very beginning like a game of poker where the cards are quickly dealt and then you just wait for the game to unfold as it has to. Quickly before the buzz wears off and the bed is revealed to be merely a clearing in the neck of the woods where Gawain was allowed to be himself for a change.

Yes, the green knight said
in response to no question—
but one night stands too
are important. This
in a little field where
a garter precariously held
the head of Gawain to
his own neck. Nevertheless
he declined this invitation
and became the question
to his own answer which
came to be asked by
Morgan le Fay

Pearl

Daniel C. Remein

for David Hadbawnik

i dreamed a pearl
that made me sad
about myself and the first few
friends in the tiles of a geodesic
dome such a poem is more like the lacèd belt
than the cup it arrives
a question of jewelry faceted
with what strings of pearl perceive
when exposed to certain affective
and cognitive background radiation
are blueprints for some highly
dreamed complicated pearled percepts

perceptive of the skinny-jeaned pearl-maiden
and dressed in jewelry and embroidery
the pearl-maiden busts coyly
into the laboratory busts up
the dreaming and standing-apace
shows the space the spirit takes
in an erlenmeyer flask about the
space of a screw-on earring
          the pearl-maiden should be a greeter
but there is no setting only force-fields
delight that eyes and ears restrain woods
like knives and invisible gem-cliffs and sharp water

hal, the thing about a gem
the setting of a gem
is the last stream
thinks you pristine
like the setting of a gem
and what is emerald is a translucent fish
with green scales
pushed out of a national forest
campground back into the back-
garden and ecological guidebooks
to this fair region (say, the adirondack peaks)
bank the poem's sloped decor

                              beyond the slant
or slope
a bivalve dome at the spot where the gem
sets the percepts strung in eurhythmy around the band
sometimes the city assembles from a mauve nacre
in an active chain and this force field has to be flung
and the more the marvel the more kind the mind
on the surface of a pearl it is
difficult to discern the difference
between a militant intention (percept)
and an atmosphere an active chain
                    arrayed in situatedness more and more

arrayed in percepts more and more
the pearl-maiden is always reciting
the elementary distinction in phenomenology
between content and act
the intentio vs. the intentum
        (without the intentio the intentum still going along
just fine again the problem of shelter
proposed by the stanza testing gilded water
the dodecahedron rafters of the pavilion
you cannot see that the pearl-maiden
rests in the very spot keeps dreaming me
that stop without in any spot

sten & robin & emily & josh, it isn't metaphorical or allegorical
that the pearl-
maiden dreams a poem without any metaphor
where the rubies at streams' edge
slice feet, the moat a situating
                              delight
      more about mathematical objects
that bind militant consciousness like
the bark of a tree on the bank resembles pearl-shine
it was carolyn expounded something else to the maiden
while the yellow-green pearl sits there in the room dropt
out of the dream about the unkindness of pearls

garland of jewels much more than kind
is thus an architectural problem like the booth
at the entry to a national park what kind of roof
should it have a belt of pearls around the head inset with the people's
delights arrayed the dream and drove me the wonder
of the stream and the miraculous waters and the invisible
force field is the out-pusht out-dropt
the poem dropt outside behind the bar in the mountains
at the pay-phone tests for water quality peerless what the pearl
does is to roll out the hole poked
in the poem by the edges of the setting into the green
garden but the pearl-maiden didn't drop

✷ ✷ ✷ ✷ ✷ ✷ ✷ ✷ ✷ ✷ ✷

the dreamer of the poem has melted brains
in the garden because the globe of a fair region breaks in
and dreams up this one
        a rock-garland   fair region
    a peerless vision arrayed
in percepts more and more the pearl is a tent
of irradiated calcium
        that poetry stretches through time

Tidy

Chris Piuma

for Sweety

Everyone loves a tidy poem.

Everyone loves a tidy poem,
a poem told in a tidy manner,
told in tiny, tidy morsels,
tightly timed in tidy lines.

Everyone loves the tidy love
a tidy poem tells us of,
of tidy manners and tiny morsels,
marked by the manner of its telling

Everyone loves a poem in which
the manner of the poem's telling
and the matter that it tells
match up in a tidy way.

Everyone loves a tidy love.

A tidy order to the dress
kindles a careful wantonness:
The hair about the shoulders combed
into a fixed attraction:
A beardless face, which here and there
Admits a crimson character:
A shirt of white, a suit of blue,
a belt that matches well the shoe:
A wholesome scent, which yet is good
beneath a long preputial hood:
A sturdy cock, whose prudent flow
will propogate the status quo:
I am enamoured by this art
that is precise in every part.

A tidy line is an ordered line.
A tidy line is a numbered line.
A tidy line is a measured line.
A tidy line is a patterned line.

A tidy line is a lucid line.
A tidy line is a limpid line.
A tidy line is a well-spelled line.
A tidy line is a well-spelt line.

A tidy line is a simple line.
A tidy line is a dimpled line.
A tidy line is a braided line.
A tidy line is a plaited line.

A tidy line is a well-kept line.
A tidy line is a well-kempt line.
A tidy line is a crystal line.
A tidy line is crystalline.

Everyone loves a tidy meal,
a square meal, at regular hours,
just proportions, evenly cooked,
and eaten among a quorum of friends.

The pound cake is a tidy cake:
        1 lb flour
        1 lb butter
        1 lb eggs
        1 lb sugar

The simple syrup is a tidy syrup:
        1 c water
        1 c sugar

The Negroni is a tidy drink:
        1 oz gin
        1 oz sweet vermouth
        1 oz Campari

A glass of water is not tidy,
for what is it in proportion to?
Likewise, a man who eats alone
is unproportioned and untidy.

But two men and two women dining,
who dip their pound cake into syrup,
who clink and drink their four Negronis:
This is very tidy indeed!

Life is a tidy food
Upon a spotless plate,
Whose table for some Guests, but not
A solo meal, is set.
Whose crumbs the waiters seek
And with a metal blade
Swipe away the maculate;
Men eat a while and die.

An even death is a tidy death:

	yrs	mos	days
Raphael, the painter	37	0	0
Kamehameha V of Hawaii	42	0	0
Juan Ponce de Leon	63	0	0
Ingrid Bergman	67	0	0
Henry I of Portugal	68	0	0
Alfred Kazin	83	0	0
Walter Diemer, inventor of bubblegum	93	0	0
Astrid Zachrison	113	0	0

Round even deaths, the more so:

Johann Ambrosius Bach, father of J.S.	50	0	0
Yasujiro Ozu	60	0	0
Constantine Cafavy	70	0	0
Bidhan Chandra Roy	80	0	0

They say that Moses, Muhammad, and Shakespeare all had tidy deaths, because they were so beloved, and this seems tidy enough to be true.

MRS. Kamlesh Vats alias Sweety born on 06-Feb-1967 at 09:005 am on Monday had shared the day of her death on 06-Feb-2012 at 09:10 am that too on Monday. She was a Pharmacist by Profession

Yet there are those who trash the tidy life!
Who bid the bare edge of a blade to cut
The flesh of any fair and faultless person,
Bash their babies, spill their blood and brains,
Crush their pets, their cats and dogs, to death,
Gash the gut and gullet of the good
To spill their stomachs in a sloppy ditch!
Who kill those who they kill, but don't kill all
Lest even killing be done tidily,
But subjugate the rest in servitude
And dank eternal toil—or leave them be,
That, for the moment unmolested, they
Might spend untidy time awaiting Trnta
                                   highl
                                   etoel
                                   winw!

                                   Amen.

Patience

Lisa Ampleman

in response to the 'Pearl' poet

Blessed are the bus riders, the wallflowers, the righteous, the pure, those who break up a bar fight, who weep for their lost, those who wield mercy like a healing balm, or endure the malice of others. They will be heaven-rich.

So, have patience. When the poet turns the virtues into Dames, vulnerable old ladies with tight snoods, and whines about his post to Rome. When he, bound to Poverty, plays with her and Patience,

>(dallies? praises? something less than pure?)

       have patience.

When the poet asks you to tarry
a little time. When he tells—for
four hundred sixty lines—the story
of Jonah (so much more than
whale bait), have patience.

When the meek are welders, torch
at hand. When you're in the
stocks, your wrists out and
vulnerable, your face an open
plate. When Tarshish is a
hundred nautical miles away.
When the wind blows the waters
so high the ship drinks them, have
                              (when the foreign,
                                useless gods
                                are women)
patience. When Jonah snores through
the storm, when he's hauled up
to deck and tossed out, when
the fish, rolling too, opens
his leviathan maw, and Jonah,
the shirker, tumbles heel over head,
                    but, as the poet
             sings,   ever is our God
        sweet.
     Have patience.

When Jonah dreams in the gullet.
And the whale is sick at heart.
                                        (when even the whale
                                                is *he*):
When God's word wails in a wind
but Jonah still pledges his troth.
When he's dropped at Nineveh's gates,
and the bachelors get the news
of their fate. When they repent,
and drop dust on their heads,
                                          (not while cleaning—
                                                not a man's job)
when that's not enough for our man.

When he sulks to a field without shade,
grumbles, (*why didn't you destroy
that whole township?*), gathers the grasses
to hide. When a woodbine twines around him,
perfect shelter, Lord-given,
and he dawdles in its perfect embrace.
When a worm, root-bane, withers the plant,
and God confronts the coward He'd coddled
                              (when we need a pronoun
                                for God).

Have patience. After all, when the city
is saved, who cares that there are fools
who can't tell their left from
their right, or accept the Lord's
judgment. Those stupid little bairns,
those unwitted women. Be naught
so gryndel, good man   (or good woman).
Have patience. In pain and in joy.

For if you rend your clothes
    (tearing blue jeans at the soft seam,
     scissoring a sock, a blouse)
you'll just have to sew them again.
The poet can suffer in silence, travel
to Rome (perhaps not, as he sees it,
a punishment), have patience.

www.ingramcontent.com/pod-product-compliance
Lightning Source LLC
Chambersburg PA
CBHW070850160426
43192CB00012B/2384